The Queen Victoria monument remains intact but the scene from Derby Square is one of total devastation

Pedestrians carry on with their business at the junction of Ranelagh Street, Renshaw Street and Lime Street. The burnt-out shell of the Lewis's building can be seen on the left

SEVENTY YEARS ON...

LIVERPOOL has had to hunker down and pull together on a number of occasions but never more so than during the May blitz of 1941.

For eight consecutive nights, the area suffered a fierce barrage as the Luftwaffe rained bombs, land mines and incendiary devices from above.

Houses, office buildings, shops, warehouses and the dockyards were flattened in an attempt to paralyse the city. It started on May 1 at 10.34pm and ended at 4.25am on May 8.

In between times, the region became warily familiar with the wail of the air-raid sirens, the drone of aircraft, the crash of anti-aircraft guns and the sickening thud of bombs as they exploded on the ground.

Liverpool, the most heavily bombed British city outside London, suffered greatly. Along with Birkenhead, it was a prime target because it was the nation's biggest west-coast port. Ships arrived every week from the USA and Canada, carrying desperately needed supplies of food and other cargo.

CONTENTS

Landmarks such as the Overhead Railway, Lewis's and Blacklers stores were devastated; Castle Street and Lord Street were all but laid to waste; factories, offices, railway lines, schools, hospitals, air-raid shelters, pubs, cinemas and churches were all targeted.

Half of the docks were put of action; 500 roads were rendered impassable; railway and tram lines were brought down; over 700 water mains and 80 sewers were badly damaged; gas, electricity and telephone services were disrupted and there were 400 separate fires to deal with on the night of May 3/4 alone.

Inevitably, such a concentration of bombing brought significant loss of life. Nearly 2,000 people were killed and over 1,000 seriously injured. Almost 100,000 homes were hit and over 75,000 people were left homeless. Fires raged and the smell of burning lingered in the air, morning, noon and night.

The region's suffering wasn't confined to eight nights in May. Serious bombing began in August 1940 and continued intermittently until January 1942 with peaks occurring during different periods. National Museums Liverpool say about 4,000 people were killed on Merseyside as a result of the Nazi attacks, including 2,736 in Liverpool, 454 in Birkenhead and 424 in Bootle.

Overall, the Luftwaffe made approximately 80 air raids on Merseyside, the intensity reaching a peak during a horrific week in May '41 that may have changed the face of the city, but didn't break its spirit.

Officials examine the wreckage of a school in Bebington, Wirral, after it experienced a direct hit

MERSEY BLITZ

Produced by Trinity Mirror Media
Business Development Director: Mark Dickinson
Executive Editor: Ken Rogers
Senior Editor: Steve Hanrahan
Editor: Paul Dove
Senior Art Editor: Rick Cooke
Sport Media Marketing Executive: Claire Brown
Sales and Marketing Manager: Elizabeth Morgan
Sales and Marketing Assistant: Karen Cadman

Mersey Blitz compiled and written by:
Alan Jewell and Harold Brough

Design/Production: Zoe Bevan, Colin Harrison, Vicky Andrews
Printed by PCP

*Pictures courtesy of the Liverpool Daily Post & Echo archive;
Liverpool Record Office; and Stewart Bale Collection, National
Museums Liverpool*

Trinity Mirror Media

© Trinity Mirror / Liverpool Daily Post & Echo

ISBN 978 1 906802 820

EIGHT NIGHTS OF HELL

In the darkest days of World War II, the full fury of the airborne forces of the greatest military machine in history was launched on Merseyside and its people

FOR eight nights in May 1941, German bombers left their bases in mainland Europe with a cargo of fire-raising incendiary bombs, high explosives and mines to be unleashed over Liverpool, particularly the docks, Britain's lifeline for supplies of food and materials from across the Atlantic.

The early years of the conflict brought war to the civilian population of Britain and in the lovely English spring of 1941, Merseyside was suddenly in the front line.

Frustrated in the attempt to invade Britain in 1940, defeated by RAF Fighter Command in the Battle of Britain in the skies over the south east, the German High Command planned a new, different offensive; an attack on the nation's industrial cities and the ports.

The plan was to destroy the British war economy and the morale of its people, with nightly air attacks. The raids continued for eight months with hardly an interruption. ➤

Above: The burnt-out shell of the famous
Blacklers store, Great Charlotte Street

Debris litters the Liverpool Palace ice rink after a bomb came through the roof in September 1940

On Merseyside, children were evacuated to safe areas outside the city, to Wales and elsewhere. Extra water supplies were arranged to fight the anticipated fire storms. Anti-aircraft gun and searchlight sites were prepared. Tens of thousands of sandbags were ordered to protect public buildings.

Houses with basements were asked to make them available as shelters. Indoor shelters were put on sale for £7.60 and, for those without DIY skills, it was suggested boy scouts could do the assembly job. Gas masks were issued and, in preparation for the likely breakdown in communications, including that caused by streets blocked with fallen masonry, messengers were recruited at £1 a week for the under 17s. The chandeliers in Liverpool Town Hall were lowered and put in storage.

Meanwhile, life went on and there was relief in football matches, dance halls and cinemas, including the Paramount where Norman Shearer and Robert Taylor starred in 'Escaped'. The Empire offered music and laughter in

'Happy Go Lucky' and at Blacklers, ladies could buy a spring suit for £2 and a gown for less than £3.

Merseyside had been under attack the year before. The first casualty was at 12.30am on August 9 1940 when a stick of bombs fell on Prenton. Twenty-four hours later seven high explosives fell in Wallasey, leaving 32 casualties.

August 31 brought the first serious attacks on the city. The Customs House was bombed, while the Sailors Home in Canning Place was machine-gunned. There were serious fires in Kings Dock, with other blazes at Queen's, Coburg, Brunswick and Wapping.

The most significant loss of life in Liverpool during the war occurred in the early hours of November 29 ➤

Left: A yawning chasm where the Shakespeare Hotel in Sir Thomas Street once stood. At the top of the page, residents carry out repairs after windows were smashed

➤ when a communal shelter below the Edge Hill Training College on Durning Road took a direct hit.

When a parachute mine hit the college, it collapsed into the shelter, crushing many of the 300 occupants. Boiling water from the central heating system and gas from fractured mains poured in. Fires made the rescue operation extremely hazardous and 166 people were killed, with many more badly injured.

The next sustained barrage occurred on the nights of December 20-21, which became known as the 'Christmas blitz'. Dozens of flares were dropped by the Luftwaffe, followed by thousands of incendiaries, land mines and high explosives. Central shopping and office districts were targeted. The Adelphi Hotel was damaged and two of the city's most famous department stores, Lewis's and Blacklers, had their windows wrecked, as did virtually every shop on Ranelagh Street, Lime Street and Renshaw Street. On the 21st, St George's Hall went up in flames and Church Street was a raging inferno.

As bad as these attacks had been, they were a prelude to the nights of horror and terror that were to come in the great May-time raids of 1941.

The first hint of the arriving war came with the drone of the bombers approaching from the west, then the whistle of the descending bombs. Then came the sounds of war; the awesome eruption of explosion and flames; the wail of sirens; the hiss of ruptured water mains; the crash of falling buildings as streets, homes, offices, shops and dockland buildings were reduced to rubble.

When the bombers turned for home they left behind unimaginable scenes of destruction across the city, smouldering wastelands where rescuers hunted for the survivors and carried away the dead.

One of the most harrowing scenes was at Mill Lane Hospital where two luggage labels were tied on the wrists of an infant. One carried the words: 'Born. May 2.' The label on the other wrist said: 'Died. May 3.' The baby's mother lay dead alongside. ➤

The bombed-out remains of warehouses and administation buildings in the docks. Liverpool was the main port of entry for war materials and food from the USA, making it a primary target for the Luftwaffe

Furniture stands in the street after these houses in Bootle were hit

Where there had been homes and streets the scene was of rubble to the far horizon. People tried to continue with their lives. The tears were of sorrow but also defiance and anger.

The city knew the attacks were coming, through intelligence from around the German airfields and the Royal Observers Corps, scanning the skies, trying to plot the bombers' course. Around the Merseyside target area the defences included radar, anti-aircraft guns, searchlights, barrage balloons over the docks and, finally, the British night fighters with formidable fire power. But all had their limitations.

Unlike the Battle of Britain, the battle of the Blitz was a night-time engagement. Coastal radar and the Observer Corps found it difficult to provide reliable information at night. The guns worked in conjunction with the searchlights but cloud and a bright moonlight could make the beams almost invisible. Anyway, if troubled by the lights, the bombers simply flew at a higher, safe altitude.

Unfortunately for Merseyside and other civilian areas in the front line, British air strategists had decided that whatever defences were prepared, it was inevitable that the bomber would reach its target. In the air war, offence was the best means of attack. So the major production and planning effort went into bombers rather than fighters.

When the bombers arrived, as the military had

thought likely, the defence rested on the men of three squadrons. Their great handicap was the lack of airborne radar to find the bombers in the darkness.

Across the centuries the river had been Liverpool's great fortune, the reason for its prosperity. In May 1941, it provided a distinctive target, particularly under a bright moon, a bomber's sky. So the destruction began, thousands died and Liverpool acquired a permanent place in wartime history – the most bombed city in England outside London.

Top left: Charred and battered, St Nicholas Church is exposed to the elements in May 1941

Above right: A prophetic warning for the Fuhrer

The Overhead Railway is brought crashing to earth near the Pier Head

THE CENTRE OF THE STORM

Huge areas of the city centre were laid to waste as the Luftwaffe unleashed a sustained barrage on the heart of Liverpool. The Overhead Railway came crashing down and iconic buildings such as Lewis's were burnt out

The 'Water Rats' from the National Fire Service fought blazes in the docks, warehouses and amongst shipping

Left: A cinema in Lime Street takes a direct hit

Below: A clearing-up operation at Mann Island

LIVERPOOL'S SCARS IN HEAVY RAIDS

HOW ST. GEORGE'S HALL SUFFERED

DAMAGE TO ADELPHI HOTEL, CHURCHES, SHOPS AND MARKET

ST. GEORGE'S HALL suffered considerable damage during a recent heavy air raid on Liverpool. The damage would have been even more widespread but for the way in which the fire bomb fighters worked. The two main courts are unharmed. Considerable damage was also sustained by the Adelphi Hotel.

IT is now possible to disclose some of the damage to well-known buildings in Liverpool during recent severe air attacks.

The most notable building to suffer was St. George's Hall, "one of the greatest edifices in the world," according to Norman Shaw, and "the finest Post-classical building in Europe" in Professor ... For nearly 100 ...

suffered considerable damage. Most of the rooms on one side, for several storeys up, were badly damaged by blast. The ballroom and grill room suffered badly, and about 200 bedrooms were rendered unusable; these are being put into a habitable condition again. The decoration of the main court, one of the largest rooms of its kind in the country, was extensively damaged, but for ... to an extent which ...

The Corn Exchange lies in ruins but these businessman carry on regardless, conducting their affairs in the open air or in nearby coffee houses

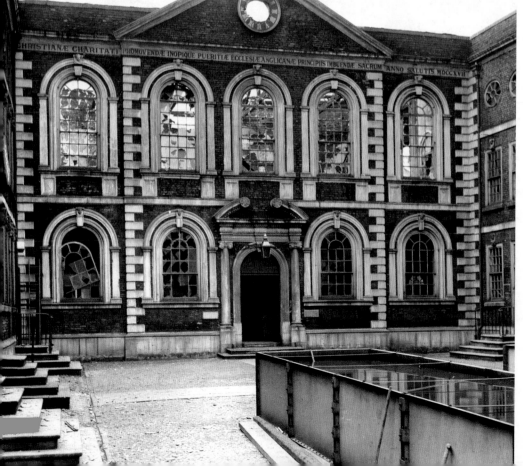

Windows smashed at the Bluecoat Chambers, the oldest building in central Liverpool

Above: Clearing up the broken glass from a shop window in September 1940. The top picture shows the smouldering ruins of the Cook Street arcade, at the junction with Castle Street, which was burnt out on the night of May 3/4

St Luke's, which will always be known in Liverpool as 'the bombed-out church', was gutted by fire on May 5

A painting of King George VI's coronation stands defiant outside the Protestant Reformers' Memorial Church, on Netherfield Road, after it was struck

SEVEN OF THE MERSEYSIDE RAIDERS DOWN

And Several Others Not Likely To Have Got Home

THRILLING BATTLE IN SKY

Heroic Rescues Of People Trapped In Debris

The ECHO learns that at least seven enemy aircraft were brought down during last night's raid on Merseyside. It is considered probable that several others failed to reach home.

IT was stated to-day by the Air Ministry and Ministry of Home Security

Boy Rescuers

Gallant Work In The Long Raid

In one Merseyside district a large number of high-explosive bombs and incendiaries were dropped, but there were no casualties and relatively little damage.

A bomb of heavy calibre fell in a working-class area and numbers of people had to be evacuated, but the Women's Voluntary Services and the civil defence organisation quickly housed them in the rest centres.

The fire-fighting services, both A.F.S. and the regular brigade, prevented any fires attaining serious proportions.

In an adjoining district considerable damage was done to house property, and there were some fatal casualties when two high-explosive bombs fell within a short distance of one another.

Fires were started, and several people were trapped in the debris of their houses.

BY TORCHLIGHT

Two women were

Above: A large hole outside TJ Hughes on London Road, which was bombed in September 1940 and May 1941

Top: The shocking scene on the morning after a raid at St Catherine's Church, Abercromby Square, on May 6.

Right: The Home Guard march down Lime Street

The twisted, mangled wreckage of the
Overhead Railway in James Street

Lord Street can be seen on the extreme right. Most
of the rest of the area has been flattened. This is now
the site of the Liverpool One shopping complex

Brunswick Street, looking towards the Pier Head. The Mersey Tunnel ventilation tower stands tall above the carnage

An improvised static water supply, created in the basement of a demolished building in Paradise Street, looking towards Bunney's Corner on Church Street

Huskisson Dock after the SS Malakand explosion on the night of May 3/4, which could be heard for miles around. A barrage balloon had become entangled in the ship's rigging and ignited. Almost immediately showers of incendiary bombs descended on those trying to clear the obstruction. The ship was manhandled off the quay but, without warning, the cargo of high explosives blew up. Some idea of the force can be gained from parts of the ship's steel plates being found two-and-a-half miles away, inside the city itself

Staff attempt to salvage some of the priceless artefacts from the Liverpool Museum on May 3

> When I arrived on duty at 5.30am on May 4, it was to find the museum in flames. The roof had collapsed and with it a lot of masonry, trapping the firemen's hoses. The main hall with the ventilator shafts and wooden beams had gone up in flames and I shall never forget seeing the flames sweeping around the galleries.

FREDERICK WILKINSON, AN ATTENDANT-WATCHMAN WITH RESPONSIBILITY FOR THE LIVERPOOL MUSEUM ON WILLIAM BROWN STREET

Above: The remains of the Philip, Son and Nephew bookshop on Church Street

Left: Emergency supplies for those left without shelter via the back of this car in Lord Street

Right: The Cook Street Aracde with a traction engine present during demolition work.

Looking down into the Lewis's building, a
pile of wire, bricks, girders and rubble

Practising with gas masks in the Liverpool telephone exchange. This building, on South John Street, was destroyed by fire during the May blitz, leaving the city without telephone services

On the night of May 3 1941, a munitions train received a direct hit in Clubmoor, causing a series of huge explosions that could be heard over a large area. A group of 10 railway employees, led by goods guard George Roberts, shunted the blazing wagons to safety, at tremendous risk to their own lives. Speaking in 1971, Mr Roberts, who was awarded the George Medal for his bravery, recalled:

66

We were in the guards' waiting room at Edge Hill when we heard that Breck Road had been bombed. We went there by train to find the place an inferno. The Auxiliary Fire Service were already there doing a great job but they were running out of water.

Huge pieces of debris were flying all over the place and the whole of the area was alight with fires. There were 32 wagons on the train, each containing at least 10 tonnes of explosives. A bomb had dropped right in the middle of the train and the ammunition in the wagons was going off like squibs. After working for some hours we managed to uncouple the wagons and shunt them into a siding. 99

BLAZING AMMUNITIO TRAIN SHUNTED

LIVERPOOL RAILWAYMEN BRAVERY RECOGNISED

Ten Liverpool railwaymen, all employed in the goods traffic department of the London Midland and Scottish Railway, who took their lives in their hands during a raid, when they carried out emergency shunting operations on a siding where an ammunition train was exploding and on fire, figure prominently in the latest list in last night's *London Gazette*.

One of them, George Roberts, aged 34, a goods guard, of 1 Hibbert Street, Liverpool, receives the George Medal, and British Empire Medals are awarded to Peter Kilshaw, aged 37, of 25 Terrace, Hale Bank, and James Edward Rowland, of Coleridge Street, Liverpool, both of them goods guards.

Train Hit By Bomb

Commendations for brave conduct in connection with the same incident go to: Drivers Robert Bate, aged 48, 11 Colville Street, Liverpool, and Alexander Ritchie, aged 63, of 30 Childwall Mount Road; Firemen William Frederick Fowler, aged 19, of 39 Wordsworth Street, Edge Hill, and George Wilkinson, aged 38, of 4 Lord Street, Bootle; Shunter Robert Owen Evans, aged 49, of 57 Daffodil Road, Liverpool, Signalman Peter William Stringer, aged 22, of Goswell Street, Liverpool, and John Guinan, aged 34, of 22 Witton Road, Liverpool a goods guard.

The story of the men's gallantry reveals complete indifference to danger while under fire from enemy bombs. One bomb hit the ammunition train, the effect being to cause fire and explo... among the wagons.

Mr George Roberts, who has awarded the George Medal, led a... who subsequently undertook dangerous shunting and uncou... operation. Acc... panied by Ja... Edward Rowla... who receives... British Em... Medal, and later by Goods Guard John Guinan, who had been off duty and had rushed to the scene from his home ... and the situation ... coupling ... began ... from those already on fire. This was continued by him in spite of repeated explosions both amid the ammunition and when bombs dropped around. He later warned householders of the danger and ushered them to safety.

Signalman Blown From His Box

Goods Guard Kilshaw, another Empire medallist, enabled shunting operations to be speeded up by entering a closed signal box and, having studied the diagrams, set the lines clear for the arrival of shunting engines. Both he and his co-medallist, James Rowland, are described as having shown "complete disregard of many dangers." The engines were brought to the point in the face of serious explosions, by ... Ritchie and Firemen...

G. ROBERTS
(GEORGE MEDAL)

The roof of a tram lies in the middle of what was then South Castle Street, before the construction of Liverpool Crown Court

Paradise Street, now the home to the Liverpool One shopping complex, was virtually flattened. Customs House, which itself was bombed more than once, stands tall in the background

Bomb-damaged offices, looking towards Liverpool Town Hall from South Castle Street

Brunswick Street, from the
junction with Fenwick Street. The
ruins of the Corn Exchange are
on the left, the rear of India
Buildings are on the right. A
curious onlooker has his eye on
the photographer.

The interior of Customs
House, which was first
bombed on August 31 1940

The rear of the Dock
Board offices

Drury Lane, looking towards James
Street. The White Star building is
shown amid the wreckage

THE BATTLE IN THE AIR

As Liverpool burned, the fight was on to restrict the enemy's bombing raids. While ARP wardens and spotters performed heroics, fighter pilots were hampered by their basic radar systems. Those defending the city from the Luftwaffe were battling against the odds

A rooftop spotter and his messenger keep an eye out for approaching aircraft

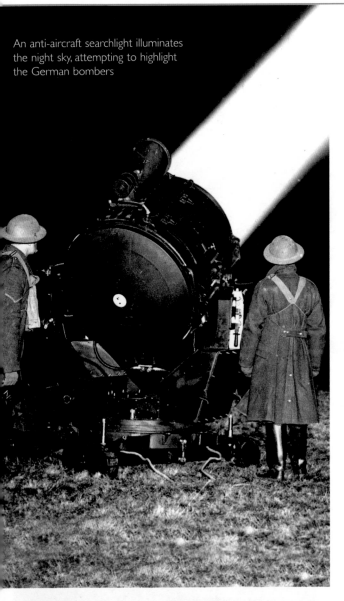

An anti-aircraft searchlight illuminates the night sky, attempting to highlight the German bombers

THE comforting sight of the air-raid shelters, anti-aircraft guns, searchlights and the airfields with night fighter squadrons positioned for the defence of Merseyside masked a terrifying reality for those who waited for the raids they knew would come.

The attack on the region was not even a difficult mission for the bomber crews.

After the defeat of France in 1940, Germany was able to move its airfields closer to the English Channel. So the Mersey was within convenient range. The pilots found their target with the aid of compass, radio beams and on moonlit nights their eyesight; on some nights the lights on the coast of neutral Ireland aided them. For most crews, the Mersey was an easy target to reach, identify and bomb, while avoiding the RAF night fighters and returning home safely. ➤

Fire watchers in training at Everton ARP (Air Raid Precautions) School

➤ Merseyside's defence depended finally on the fighter planes of the RAF. But night fighting was a relatively new kind of war. The planes were designed for daytime operations. Despite some minor conversions, the problems for the pilots, searching for bombers in the blackness of the vast skies, were so immense many German crews discharged their load over the city and the docks before returning home without meeting even one night fighter during the entire week of the blitz.

Luftwaffe bomber pilot Diether Lukesch reported: "Actually the defences were quite strong. But it was a big target and easy to find." Lukesch piloted a dive bomber, putting his plane in a dive from 12,000 feet, hurling towards the docks and the ships at 550 mph. knowing that with G-forces at least five times above normal he would pass out, briefly.

At 6,000 feet he released the bombs and, consciousness returning, turned the bomber inland, away from the illuminating fires of the city to the sanctuary of the darkness. He was 23, a lieutenant.

Among his friends in the bomber squadrons, Gunther Unger had been shot down the previous year and ditched in the Channel but was back in action for the blitz on Merseyside. He explained: "Liverpool was one of the easiest targets. You could hardly miss it. We never had one definite target. We

Above: An unexploded landmine. The top picture shows Mr and Mrs Clague, who had been saved by their Anderson shelter

A firefighter tackles an
incendiary bomb

The Salvage Squad search through the bomb-damaged remains of terrace housing. They helped home owners recover personal belongings and recycled any raw materials that were available

What to do next? This rescue worker contemplates the scale of the job ahead

The Women's Voluntary Service hand out hot drinks to grateful Merseysiders

were ordered to bomb the docks. There was a map in our briefing room with a line marking out the area and we bombed inside that. It did not matter whether we hit a ship, dock or warehouse. They were all important."

The reasons why many bombs fell outside the target area, including residential districts, were many. Barrage balloons and the anti-aircraft guns prevented low-level bombing and were successful in their roles of forcing the bombers to high altitude. Weather and wind speed varied from the forecasts. Bomb-aiming devices were imperfect and G-forces could affect the pilot's aim. If a bomber came under the guns of a night fighter it was usual for the bombs to be released immediately and indiscriminately, in the desperate attempt to escape. Also, bombers were sometimes fooled into bombing on the decoy fires lit far from the docks. Unger was shot down again. He had just released his bombs when he saw his starboard engine on fire. The Junkers was doomed and he ordered the crew to bail out, following them through the hatch, drifting westwards on the wind and splashing down in the sea.

A father and daughter, both injured during a raid on their home, salvage some of their belongings as they are re-housed

➤ With his parachute canopy above and filled with air, he could not inflate his life-jacket. He swallowed a lot of water and his strength was ebbing fast. Suddenly, joyously, he found he was in just four feet of water. He had landed in sandbanks off Wirral. He walked and waded through the mud and water, heading towards the flames and explosions over the city. More than an hour later, exhausted, he struggled ashore on Wallasey beach and surrendered to a surprised Home Guardsman.

The incoming bombers were identified early on radar. But after crossing the English coast most of the flight north was not covered by radar. Their detection relied on the Royal Observer Corps (ROC) actually seeing the planes. Wartime premier Winston Churchill described the transition as like moving from the middle of the 20th century to the early stone age.

The ROC tried to assess the numbers, route and height of the bombers, a difficult job by day and often impossible at night. But they sent advance warning for the fighter controllers to prepare to put the planes airborne. The decision had to be carefully judged. If the fighters were sent up too soon to wait for the bombers they could waste fuel. Sometimes the decision was delayed so long the bombers were already dropping their loads before the fighters were over the target area.

The fighters were the bombing crews' great fear. The fate of Merseyside depended on the pilots of three squadrons, based near Shrewsbury, Holmes Chapel and Blackpool, equipped with Hurricanes, Defiants, Bristol Blenheims and Beaufighters.

They were directed to their targets with the help, limited at the time, of ground radar. But the great deficiency was that only one of the squadrons is known to have had airborne radar and that was early rudimentary equipment. Mostly it was a matter of the fighter pilots seeing a bomber in the night sky. ➤

Top picture: An ARP fire engine amongst bomb-damaged suburbs on Merseyside. In the image immediately above, an Anderson shelter can be seen in the middle of the picture. These came in kit form and were made of corrugated iron. Once assembled, a hole was dug and the shelter sunk into the hole. The shelter was then covered with earth

A control car used by the Auxilary Fire Service during the Blitz

Toddlers get used to wearing gas masks

❝Airbone radar was rudimentary. Mostly it was a matter of the fighter pilots seeing a bomber in the night sky❞

Damage to houses (left) and a factory after more enemy raids

➤ RAF ground stations could detect bombers on radar. But without airborne radar the fighter pilots flew over the target areas, along imaginary corridors at 500 feet intervals, in circles at heights of 500 to 2,000 feet, simply hoping to see a bomber against the backcloth of the city in flames, or caught in the glare of a searchlight or silhouetted against the moon. If they were lucky they would sometimes see the sparks from a bomber's exhaust.

The fighter pilots became known as the Cats Eyes squadrons and, between missions of great danger in the black night, they tried to improve their night vision. At the airfields their operational readiness rooms had low-level lighting and they wore goggles with dark lenses so their eyes would adjust to the darkness in the combat area. Their planes too had cowlings put over the engines so that a spark would not cause any interruption to their night vision.

Robin McNair was among these brave young men and when asked about the success of these operations, he said: "The interception rate was very low. It was an uphill battle all the way. It is not surprising so many bombers got through.

"Without radar it was difficult. But not as hard as it might seem. Sometimes you would see the moon glinting on the body of a bomber or see one against the clouds or stars. Or if you were close you could see the spurts from the red-hot exhaust. People imagine waves of bombers but usually we saw only one at a time. The sky is a big place. If you saw the one plane you attacked that."

His victims included a Heinkel flying south after releasing its bombs. McNair turned his Hurricane in pursuit and, positioned below and behind the bomber, remained hidden against the dark earth while the bomber was silhouetted against the lighter sky.

From 80 yards McNair, with his gunner, fired two, four-second bursts from the eight guns. The bomber began trailing smoke and its fuel tanks burst open, covering the Hurricane in oil. The fighter fired again as the crippled bomber began to dive. The Heinkel crashed in flames near Widnes.

McNair became famous locally and some of the traders at Middlewich, where he had lodgings, gave his family extra rations. But he did not feel like a celebrity. He never went to see his kill. "I was never interested in seeing crashed planes, not when you think of what it means," he said.

McNair, then 22, operated from Cranage, near ➤

The Home Guard in training. They were originally known as the Local Defence
Volunteers and comprised people ineligible for military service

"The awful reality was that the defences were never adequate; destruction and death were almost inevitable "

► Holmes Chapel, and patrolled over the docks. He had no difficulty in finding the combat zone at night. "When I got near I did not need a compass," he said. "The whole place was in flames, a horrifying sight. I simply flew towards the flames."

He thought he destroyed two, possibly three bombers in defending the city and the docks. But then on the best nights for the RAF night fighters, only a small proportion of the enemy were destroyed and mostly they bombed unhindered.

McNair survived the war and went to work for British Airways. Unger remained a prisoner of war until 1946 when he returned to Germany and started an engineering business.

"Sometimes we did feel frustrated we had not been more successful against the bombers, particularly when we were up and over the area a good time before they arrived," said McNair. "I remember feeling mighty sorry for the city and its people."

The awful reality was that the defences were never adequate; destruction and death were almost inevitable, once the bombers had the river in their sights, ideally for them, bright in the moonlight.

The city and the docks were effectively exposed. Indeed many bombers came in from the west, from over the sea. As Sir Richard Pile, head of the Anti Aircraft Command, put it, the defence of Merseyside from that direction was "almost impossible".

The Royal Ordnance Factory in Kirkby. By the summer of 1941, 10,000 people were employed, rising to a peak of 20,000, most of whom were women. Production was maintained 24 hours a day

A family was killed when this house was hit in Waterloo

These workmen are virtually below ground level in this giant crater

Jets of water attempt to quell a huge fire at
Alexandra Dock after a night-time raid

WHEN BOOTLE BURNED

Proportionate to its size, Bootle was the most bombed area in Britain. The proximity of the docks made it a target for the Luftwaffe and residential areas suffered greatly. It's estimated that between 65% and 85% of its houses were destroyed during the air raids

A large hole exposes the
Stanley Road canal bridge

A piano stands in the street after a row of houses was all but obliterated

THE prelude to the approaching war came suddenly on a spring night, the awesome sounds of the sirens across the river, the rhythmic pounding of the anti-aircraft guns and the whistle of the bombs and the crash of falling buildings.

The day would come when the advances in radar and night fighters would make possible great losses on the enemy. But, for Merseyside under the tumbling bombs, that time was not yet.

The date was May 1, 1941, the time, 10.43 pm, the beginning of a week of bombing raids in Germany's desperate attempt to put a stranglehold on Britain war's defence and sever her vital sea routes westward across the Atlantic.

Some were able to see the planes in the light of that spring night. A voluntary fire-fighter reported: "We stood on a railway footbridge at Little Sutton and watched the bombers following the line of the Mersey towards the docks and the city.

"It was so quiet we could hear the bomb doors opening and awful, chain-like sounds, like something falling into place. Then we knew the bombs would soon be released."

"The planes came over continuously, in what seemed like droves. Across the river at Liverpool we saw the flashing of the guns and the hundreds of searchlights sweeping the sky."

The raid of May 1 was not particularly severe, about 50 bombers. The second night brought a full moon and more than 60 planes in an attack lasting over four hours. Bootle's terrible ordeal began.

May 3 brought the greatest attack of the week, 300 bombers, dropping tons of high explosives, fire-raising incendiary bombs and mines for four and a half hours. Mercifully, the raids eased for the next three nights. Then the bombers attacked in force yet again. ➤

The communal air-raid shelter in Stafford Street is still standing but surrounding houses have taken a direct hit

A chaotic scene in Cyprus Road

Millers Bridge was partially demolished

An emergency food convoy for local residents who had been bombed out of their homes

Communication was difficult with the bombing and the damage, and most messages were carried by messenger lads on bicycles. We used to carry messages from the fire station to the pumps engaged on a fire and bring back a reply, perhaps giving a brief report of the fire situation and whether reinforcements were needed. During the blitz I was on duty for eight days, sleeping on the floor in the station. Relief fire brigades were being sent to Bootle from various parts of the country. One of our jobs as messengers was to meet the incoming brigades on the outskirts of the town and guide them in and to various jobs. We would put our bicycles on the fire engines and sit beside the driver. Naturally there was fear, but this was mostly banished by the excitement of it all. And at that age it was exciting. "

RON HEYS, A 15-YEAR-OLD MESSENGER FOR THE FIRE SERVICE IN BOOTLE AT THE TIME OF THE MAY BLITZ
(16 WAS THE MINIMUM AGE FOR THIS VOLUNTARY ROLE BUT RON HAD LIED ABOUT HIS AGE)

Rescue workers inspect the remains of a house in Rimrock-Street

➤ The dock became a line of flames, a raging inferno. Homes, offices, factories and churches collapsed in piles of rubble or remained just as gaunt skeletons. Walton Prison and Hospital were hit. The Royal Daffodil II was sunk at Seacombe landing stage.

At Marsh Lane mortuary almost 200 dead were incinerated in a bomb blast and the remains buried in a communal grave at Bootle. Thousands were injured and made homeless. Entire streets of terraced houses, mostly the homes of dockers and factory workers, became piles of rubble and splinters.

More than 1,700 died on Merseyside, including 1,453 in Liverpool and more than 250 in Bootle, the most bombed town in Britain, outside of London and relative to its size. ➤

> "They died in explosions and flames; in the streets; in their collapsed homes amid falling masonry. Some died from the effects of bomb blast"

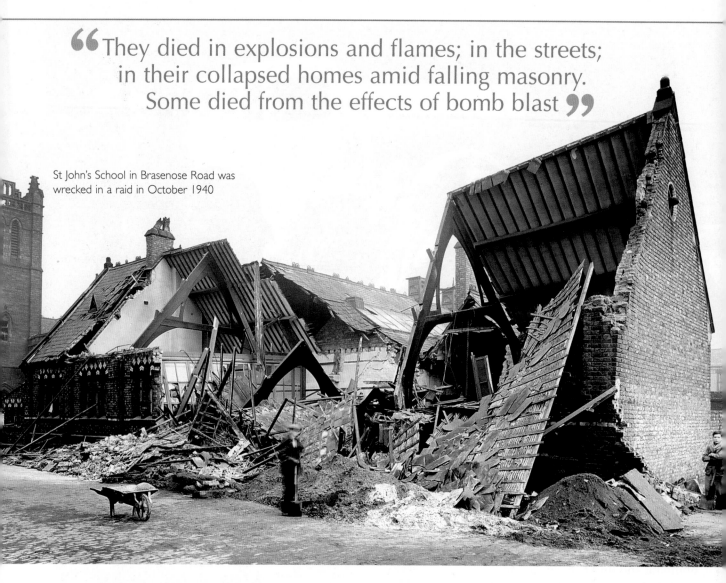

St John's School in Brasenose Road was wrecked in a raid in October 1940

➤ They died in explosions and flames; in the streets; in their collapsed homes amid falling masonry. Some died from the effects of bomb blast or, as a rescuer said after finding the bodies of two girls who died together as they reached a shelter, "the life was simply sucked out of them". Some, including the old, died from heart attacks and sheer terror.

But there were also some amazing stories of survival. Among the dead and dying the night Mill Lane Hospital was hit, surrounded by the falling walls and the cries of the injured, a young girl entered the last stage of labour, encouraged to hurry with the new life by a nurse ignoring the chaos around her.

Ken Oliver's young life was saved twice in one night. He was 15, a part-time fire brigade messenger based at the Knowsley Road station where he slept in the basement, listening to the music from the dance hall above. The few perks of the job included the uniform of a fireman, an axe and, in a time when food was rationed, a free breakfast of bacon and egg.

He was asked to take a message to the fire station at Strand Road and set off through the fires on his bicycle. "I was pedalling as fast as I could when suddenly there was a chuffing noise, like a train, and a mighty explosion," he said. "I was flung over the handlebars – I didn't half go – and landed on my back in the road. I had only left the fire station three minutes earlier and it had had a direct hit. It was just a pile of rubble."

He started walking and again heard the dreaded chuffing-train sound. The blast lifted him off his feet. He could hear people screaming and moaning in a shelter. Someone told him a boiler had burst and people were being scaled and frantically he helped clear the rubble blocking the entrance. Inside, among about 100 men, women and children, he found the girl he would marry.

A 14-year-old girl who had sheltered there with her parents every night said: "The screaming was unmerciful. The place just caved in. It was chaos, no lights, people fumbling around in the dark, shouting and screaming. It was bad that night in Bootle. Terrible. Ferocious."

Above: Windows smashed but the structure is still standing in the top picture, while below it are houses in Trinity Road that experienced more severe damage

St Andrew's Church Hall in Linacre Road, which was being run as an emergency rest centre, was hit as the canteen staff were preparing breakfast. Five Women's Voluntary Service Staff and 37 local people, many of them homeless, were killed.

On the night of May 3, the Bryant and May Matchworks factory in Litherland was hit by a series of high explosives and incendiaries. The resulting fire could be seen from North Wales and the Leeds-Liverpool canal was used as an auxiliary water supply to fight the conflagration. The factory, where 900 people were then employed, was destroyed, never to reopen, but, remarkably, nobody died. Several hundred people, mainly women and children, were in an air-raid shelter in the basement of the building on the west side of the factory. All were safely evacuated.

Wartime auxiliary nurse Nell Hopkins, on duty at Mill Lane Hospital that week, also escaped almost certain death twice within less than an hour.

Five months earlier the hospital had the most amazing luck. An air raid left the nurses' home in ruins. But the bomb had fallen during the changeover of shifts. There was not one casualty.

But in May, on the night of one of the heaviest raids on Britain, and as the hospital prepared to receive casualties from around the city, bombs fell on those already sick and the injured recovering from earlier raids.

Nurse Hopkins left the maternity ward with a cheerful goodnight to the mothers and their new babies. Just minutes later, it was hit. She reckoned there were about 30 mothers and infants in the ward and that perhaps two survived. ➤

Later that same night she was in the ambulance station waiting for her turn to go on duty. When the call came, she stepped outside into the ambulance and heard a rumbling noise. Looking back towards the station, she saw the bricks and debris falling.

Before she went on duty that night, she had been to a church fellowship meeting where she told a friend. "Don't forget to pray for me. I am on ambulance duty tonight." In the years ahead she reflected on her survival and thought of the moment she left the maternity ward with the babies who had just minutes to live. Nell Hopkins wrote many Christian poems. "I think God must have spared me for some purpose," she said.

In the basement theatre, a Greek seaman with a perforated ulcer had just been anaesthetised; the first incision made when a parachute mind landed.

A nurse recalled: "Everything was falling in. There was a slab of stone across my body and the operating table was tilted, like a sea-saw. There was a nurse who had fallen through the hole into the basement. She was hysterical, clutching her head and crying she could not see." The seaman dug out from the wreckage survived but was later lost at sea.

The bombing of the hospital was the biggest single disaster of the May blitz. It was also the most pointless. It did not damage Britain's war effort by halting the production of a single bomb or damage the docks. But 30 patients died along with 17 staff and 14 ambulance drivers. Seventy were seriously injured.

But just occasionally the bombers got lucky. The destruction of the ammunition ship the Malakand was fortunate, in military terms probably the greatest German success of the entire blitz.

During one night of massive bombardment, a single barrage balloon, loosened from its mooring and partly deflated, tumbled down towards the river. It could have landed anywhere, harmlessly, but it landed on the deck of the Malakand and immediately burst into flames. Seamen and firefighters watched horrified. The freighter carried 1,000 tonnes of high explosives destined for the armies in the Middle East.

The firemen fought the flames. But with incendiaries also dropping on the deck, and flames from the blazing dockside buildings jumping the gap to start fires the length of the ship, the situation was desperate. With flames flicking around the ammunition, the Malakand, effectively a huge ticking time-bomb, was abandoned.

> **"** We had our own fire brigade and a first-class sprinkler system. But the place flared up before anyone could do anything. Imagine the high explosives and incendiaries falling on all that highly-flammable material. Fire was raging through the premises in a matter of minutes. On top of all this, the water supply failed. Apparently a bomb had fallen on a nearby pawnbroker's shop and illuminated the factory. Next thing, these bombs were coming down like rain. **"**

JOSEPH JONES, WORKED AT BRYANT AND MAYS' FACTORY FOR 50 YEARS AND WAS A MATCH MACHINIST DURING THE WAR

On the night of May 3 1941, the Bryant and May Matchworks factory in Litherland was hit. The resulting fire could be seen from North Wales and the Leeds-Liverpool canal was used as an auxilary water supply to fight the resulting conflagration. Linacre Mission can be seen in the background

Damage to the gasworks

Houses, factories and warehouses were flattened on Rimrose Road

A shelter takes a hit on Garfield Street

"Within the families of Merseyside, the legacy of lives lost and the sadness continues even today"

Destruction in Merton Road

The inevitable blast shook the earth for miles. The roar was heard on the far side of Wirral and 20 miles away at Southport. Five miles away, at St Patrick's Church, Liverpool 8, the problem of the door being jammed by a fault in the hydraulics was solved when it was blasted back on its hinges.

The stern end of the Malakand, weighing about 50 tons, was found 30 yards away. A four-ton anchor was hurled 100 yards. Steel plates were found more than three miles away. The blitz produced many miracles of lives somehow saved. The Malakand was perhaps the greatest. The death toll was four.

Ships and buildings could be rebuilt, as could the tens of thousands of houses destroyed or damaged. Not much remains to show the blitz ever happened.

But, within the families of Merseyside, the legacy of lives lost and the sadness continues even today. Images portray the reality of the real cost of the blitz greater than statistics.

Even the temporary mortuaries filled with bodies. One 20-year-old girl, who worked as a joiner making trestles for the coffins, said: "Everything was covered in blood and there was a woman who had to wash the bodies. She had to sort out the bits and pieces.

"You have to remember that many were blown from here to kingdom come. She had to try and match pieces together before the bodies were buried. Yes, a terrible job. But it was a terrible, terrible time."

TARGET WIRRAL

The first bombs dropped on Merseyside fell on Thurstaston, Irby and Neston in July 1940. Wallasey and Birkenhead were to suffer significant damage and loss of life during the blitz

The roof and windows are blown out at Wallasey Town Hall

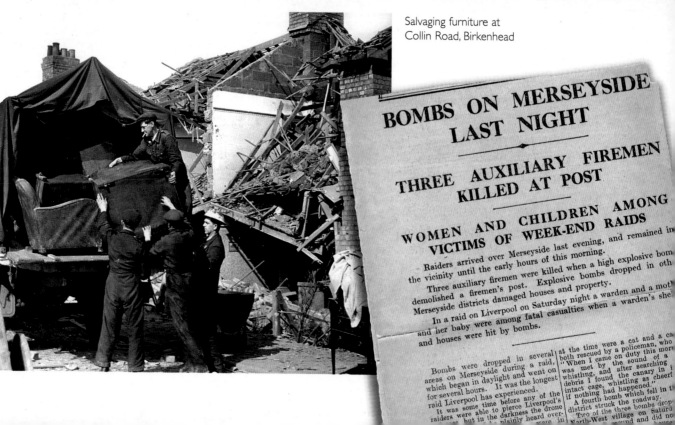

Salvaging furniture at Collin Road, Birkenhead

BOMBS ON MERSEYSIDE LAST NIGHT

THREE AUXILIARY FIREMEN KILLED AT POST

WOMEN AND CHILDREN AMONG VICTIMS OF WEEK-END RAIDS

Raiders arrived over Merseyside last evening, and remained in the vicinity until the early hours of this morning.

Three auxiliary firemen were killed when a high explosive bomb demolished a firemen's post. Explosive bombs dropped in other Merseyside districts damaged houses and property.

In a raid on Liverpool on Saturday night a warden and a mother and her baby were among fatal casualties when a warden's shelter and houses were hit by bombs.

Bombs were dropped in several areas on Merseyside during a raid, which began in daylight and went on for several hours. It was the longest raid Liverpool has experienced.

It was some time before any of the raiders were able to pierce Liverpool's ... but in the darkness heard over-...

at the time were a cat and a can... both rescued by a policeman, who ... "When I came on duty this mor... was met by the sound of a ... whistling, and after searching ... debris I found the canary in ... intact cage, whistling as cheer... if nothing had happened."

A fourth bomb which fell in t... district struck the roadway, ... Two of the three bombs drop... North-West village on Satu...

Hoylake Congregational Church was damaged in 1940

The force of an explosion blew a
car into the garden of this property
in Brougham Road, Seacombe

Winston Churchill visits the Cammell Laird shipyard

A house is virtually flattened in Henry Street, Birkenhead

Onlookers contemplate the destruction in Livingstone Street, Birkenhead

Birkenhead flour mill comes crashing down after being hit by a bomb

Boys will be boys: Having fun in a damaged field in Wallasey

An injured man watches on as a family member is rescued from an underground shelter

All the vehicles have been wrecked at a car depot in Birkenhead

A few boys closely inspect a giant
crater at Hamilton Square, Birkenhead

A house blown apart in Bebington

School children being
evacuated in Edge H[ill]

BATTERED BUT NOT BROKEN

The outlying districts of Liverpool felt the full force of the air attacks but its people were unbowed, despite the huge loss of life and shattered infrastructure. Merseyside pulled together, demonstrating courage and defiance in the most trying circumstances imaginable

THE mornings brought scenes of unimaginable destruction and chaos, a city with its heart in ruins, its people shocked, frightened, bewildered, yet grimly determined and defiant.

Fires raged across Merseyside, even in the suburbs where many had retreated from the horrors of the hours of darkness, laden with bedding to seek refuge in the fields and woods or just by the roadside. They returned in the mornings, ghost-like figures in the mist and drifting smoke. On the Liverpool side of the Mersey 100,000 homes were destroyed or damaged.

In the four boroughs of Liverpool, Bootle, Wallasey and Birkenhead, almost 1,440 died and 1,154 were seriously injured. Nearly half of the dead in Liverpool remained unidentified because complete families perished, total streets obliterated. Sometimes in packed communities when the mains burst, the water ran over the dead, dying and maimed. By the time it reached the gutter, it was stained red.

"I supposed at times there would be 100 fires burning," said Tom Kelly, then Liverpool's deputy chief fire officer.

➤

" People returned to their homes, ghost-like figures in the mist and drifting smoke **"**

"
My uncle came into our shelter looking for Mr Robinson, a neighbour. His daughter was in the college shelter and it was such a bad night's raid she was worried about him and wanted him to be with her. I'll never forget watching as my uncle led him away. That was the last time we saw them. **"**

STAN SMART, 12 AT THE TIME OF THE DURNING ROAD BOMBING

Top picture: The aftermath of the Durning Road tragedy in November 1940, when an underground communal shelter in Edge Lane was hit, killing 166 people and badly injuring many more. It was the worst loss of life in a single incident during the Liverpool blitz

Left: A huge pile of debris in Woolton

➤ The demand for water was so great that at times the jets were reduced to a trickle. Smashed mains added to the water shortage. The problems included a shortage of unskilled labour. Where it was available it lacked organisation and leadership. Fire engines struggled through roads blocked by debris and vehicles with hooded headlights made visibility limited. One fire engine fell into a bomb crater. The first fireman to die fell into the docks.

"Sometimes we thought we were fighting a losing battle, that the entire city would go up in flames," said Tom Kelly. Many worked to the point of exhaustion and beyond. Kelly, like others, never went to bed the entire week of the May blitz. One lady said: "We had little or no sleep that week. But then you had to take it as your duty, like your parents did during the 1914-18 war."

But the city and its people were not defeated. The courage and spirit of the people remained high and the city remained open for business. With transport halted and disrupted many walked great distances to work or hitched lifts in passing vehicles.

The terror and sadness revealed a sense of unity, the best of the human spirit, countless acts of self-sacrifice, courage and kindness. Those in distress and great need found help from neighbours who cleared the rubble, provided sandwiches and tea, plus shelter and longer-term rehousing. The aid agencies also acted quickly. Three people, over 80 years of age, found in the wreckage of their homes were rehoused the same day in Shropshire.

Lancashire miners arrived with picks and shovels to dig in the wreckage of homes. Two soldiers dragged a piano out of a bombed store and began playing: "There'll Always Be An England." The Liverpool Echo reported that people were not despairing but rather philosophical with the attitude: "Something like this was bound to happen sooner or later."

So under the falling bombs people listened to their radios, sang in the shelters and some went dancing to the big-band sounds. "We were teenagers hell-bent on having a good time," said one lady. "We went dancing at the Grafton in Liverpool, the Tower at New Brighton and danced until the sirens went.

"One night on the way home I was caught out during a raid. We weaved our way to the north end of Birkenhead, diving in and out of shelters in the side streets. We found cheerful faces. 'Would you like a cup of tea, love? Stay here until the all-clear.'"

Police, civil defence workers, firemen, wardens and others carried out many acts of great courage, including working among buildings on fire and in danger of collapse. The police were awarded two George Medals and three British Empire Medals. One officer was awarded a bar to his BEM, effectively the award for the second time.

An inspector was awarded a Croix de Guerre for ➤

Two policemen survey the damage to a corner house

A bath hangs perilously at this house in Anfield

gallantry for moving high explosives from a blazing Belgian ship. Some gave their lives trying to help others. The charred remains of three first-aid workers were found in the ruins of one building, apparently killed trying to rescue those trapped in the flames.

An official report suggested the battle in the air had been a draw or even a victory for the enemy "who must be admitted to have come off very lightly".

But the bombers failed to halt the production of war materials or destroy the morale of the people. Most importantly, they failed in their major objective: the destruction of the docks and cargoes and the sealing of the port.

Ships were damaged or sunk, contents were destroyed, dock gates and basins smashed. Yet much of dockland worked as normal and the port soon recovered. In the week before the May blitz 145,000 tonnes were landed. At the end of the week of raids that figure had slumped to 35,000 tonnes. But within one month the docks were handling 108,000 tonnes. One week later the figure was 126,000 and the graph was moving upward.

As the Ministry of Home Security, in a survey of Merseyside, reported: "Effective damage has not been serious in relation to the national war effort."

The people, with defiance and courage, played a major part in that achievement. The Lord Mayor, Alderman Sir Sydney Jones, told a city council meeting: "I think I can say without boasting but with great pride that Liverpool has stood up enormously well to its task…I have been amazed at the way our citizens have gone about their lives in the wanton destruction."

Liverpool's great salvation came when the raids stopped. Germany had become preoccupied with the war on the Eastern Front. If that had not happened then, as one British commander put it: "There can be no doubt at all that if the series of raids had continued, Merseyside would have been useless for a long time."

Merseyside and its people survived, recovered and so perhaps, it might be said, even won. But as was said about Waterloo: "It was a near run thing."

Only the gable end walls survive at these properties in Ardleigh Road, Edge Lane

Officials contemplate the task ahead after Arkwright Street in Everton was bombed

THE SPIRIT OF MERSEYSIDE
GREAT MEMORIES, GREAT BOOKS AND MAGAZINES . . .

Only £2.50 + £1 p&p (UK)

BATTLE OF BRITAIN

Marks the 70th anniversary of the conflict and celebrates the heroism of those who defended the nation.

DUMMY BULLETS

Sergeant Wally Huntley reveals how entertainment became the secret weapon of war.

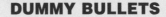

£3.50 + £1 p&p (UK)

Only £1.00 + £1 p&p (UK)

IT'S WAR

From the Daily Mirror archives – how the nation came together during World War II.

Only £3.99 + £1 p&p (UK)

LOST CINEMAS OF LIVERPOOL

Book your ticket for a trip down movie memory lane, to a time when Liverpool was a Tinsel Town in its own right and there was a cinema on every corner.

Only £2.00 + £1 p&p (UK)

THE WAY WE WORKED

Unilever, Vernons, Littlewoods, Crawford's, Tate & Lyle, Woolies. Our jobs – our memories.

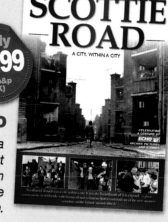

Only £3.99 + £1 p&p (UK)

SCOTTIE ROAD

The bricks and mortar of Scottie Road may be a memory but the spirit lingers on. Featuring great photographs from the Scottie Press collection and rarely seen historical images from the League of Welldoers' Lee Jones Collection.

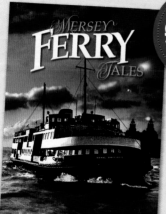

Only £3.99 + £1 p&p (UK)

MERSEY FERRIES

A collection of magic maritime memories, from the 'Fish & Chip' boats of the Sixties to the brave ferries who became a Royal Family in their own right.

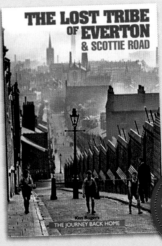

THE LOST TRIBE OF EVERTON & SCOTTIE ROAD

This nostalgic book by Ken Rogers will take you back 'home' into the inner city streets and make you feel proud.

Only £9.99 FREE p&p (UK)

To order call: 0845 143 0001 or visit MERSEYSHOP.COM

Offers while stocks last. Prices subject to change.

A parachute mine
flattens a large area
of Walton Road

A mine causes havoc near
Everton Valley

A major search, rescue and clean-up operation is underway in a number of areas on Lace Street, near Byrom Street, Scotland Road, with tenements visible on the brooding skyline

People mill around this shattered building, which was home to shops, on Vienna Street, Anfield,

Chaos all around as the wreckage still smoulders

Civilians and rescue workers pick their way through the rubble after a number of houses were flattened

The end of this block of flats has been ripped away by the force of a blast

An unexploded parachute mine proves an unexpected guest in this garden

Rescue workers search amongst the rubble in Sidney Place, Edge Hill

The interior of Walton Prison is mangled after taking a hit

A policeman stands guard close to County Road, which has been devastated by a parachute mine

A bomb has gone through the roof
of this school assembly hall

L'pool's Most Serious "Blitz"

Shops, Hotels And Churches Hit

MERSEYSIDE had its longest and most serious air "blitz" on Saturday night. Wave after wave of enemy raiders swept over the district, and in the later stages of the attack, some of them dived to drop their bombs. Considering the ferocity of the onslaught, the casualties and damage to property were singularly small. The chief facts of the raid were:

commercial, and business two hotels and were some of the buildings in the city by incendiary explosive bombs. members of the clerical staff of Catholic church and several including a soldier s Grant, who was home Shelter in the clubroom the church. The priests O'Keefe and Four people in the escued. There were in several houses church.

explosive bombs, and residents fought hundreds of incendiaries in the streets. One well-known building was fired, and as a precautionary measure hundreds of people in the shelter beneath shelters were evacuated to other

es in other parts of molished by

a suburban s wrecked, and side of the roa rage forms the c amage. Many people scapes from injury eltered.

Gallant rescue work when seven houses and eig were completely wrecked in a par icularly crowded area. Several

Treasured possessions are
ruined in a mansion bedroom

Is it okay to come out now? A group of people emerge from a shelter in Salop Street, Walton, after a raid

The house might have had the frontage ripped away but these residents can still smile thanks to the Anderson shelter which saved their lives

A University of Liverpool laboratory is wrecked by a bomb

"

It is a great crisis in our history. I suppose that never in the history of Liverpool, even in its palmist days, has the attention of the whole world been more concentrated upon it than it is now.

I think I can say, without boasting, but with great pride, that Liverpool has stood up extremely well to its task. We need steadfastness, courage, foresight, and we are glad to find these qualities prevailing throughout the city. We still have that unshaken belief in the ultimate victory. I have been amazed at the way in which our citizens have gone about their business during the past few days. We have lost a number of important buildings that are a real loss because they enshrine the history of Liverpool within her walls – they represent hundreds of years of our development as a democratic body and municipal power. We deeply deplore that a large number of our citizens have lost their lives as a result of wanton destruction. We remember those who have suffered and died. We ought to express our gratitude in our sympathy for others, to all the members of our staff and forces, voluntary or otherwise, who have so nobly come forward and played their part. I feel personally very proud today for the way in which the city has carried on. "

THE LORD MAYOR,
ALDERMAN SIR SYDNEY JONES, MAY 7 1941

Another damaged shelter in Stevenson Street, Wavertree

A street shelter in Tuebrook has superficial damage but the road is a mess

Liverpool stands together

IT'S a monument to what Merseyside endured during the blitz, and how the region survived the barrage, despite the terrible damage inflicted upon it.

St Luke's – the bombed-out church – is pictured under a moonlit sky, from where German bombers wreaked havoc on Liverpool and surrounding districts.

The May blitz of 1941 was the city's darkest hour but also, somehow, an experience in which it could take great pride.

The Luftwaffe dropped their worst but Liverpool could not be broken.

Bombs fell in a 17-month period, reaching a terrifying peak during eight nights at the start of May when huge areas were flattened and fires raged across Merseyside.

Despite the devastation to housing, shopping areas, offices, the docks, warehouses and infrastructure, not to mention the huge death toll, the Liverpool people pulled together and got on with their lives.

The spirit of the blitz saw them through.

AIR RAIDS ON LIVERPOOL

Listings from the Liverpool Record Office — see map on page 83

ABBREVIATIONS

P - Lights out message
R - Alert
W - Raiders Passed

H.E. - High Explosive bomb(s)
I.B. - Incendiary bomb(s)
P.M. - Parachute mine(s)
U.X.B. / U.X.P.M. - Unexploded bomb(s)/mine(s)

Warnings	Brief Survey of Incidents		
17/18 Aug 1940. R. 00.38 W. 02.29	12 H.E. on Brunswick, N. Coburg, S. Queens Docks damaging railway station, grain silo, water mains. Ship overturned. Slight damage.	12/13 Sept. R. 19.27 W. 21.23	H.E., S.W. Langton Dock buildings damaged. H.E. Wellington Road, two dwelling houses demolished. House in Carnatic Road extensively damaged by I.B.
19/20 Aug. P. 02.18 R. 02.19 W. 02.59	I.B. on Eaton Road district mostly on open ground. Small fires, Robert Davies Nursing Home and house property. Slight damage.	14 Sept R. 20.26 W. 20.31	One aircraft over city. H.E. and I.B. caused very slight damage to North Docks, Gladstone and Alexandra.
28/29 Aug. R. 23.50 W. 04.20	Many H.E. and I.B. dropped. Parish Church, Mossley Hill, seriously damaged by H.E. Some houses and a garage destroyed, Kingsmead Drive and St. Anne's Road, Aigburth.	15/16 Sept. P. 22.34 R. 22.37 W. 00.41	H.E. on Anfield, Fairfield, Walton and Norris Green districts and also on Speke Air Port Field. Palace Ice Rink severely damaged. House in Huntley Road demolished. Delayed action bomb exploded 12.00 hours, 16.9.40, and killed one R.A.F. officer and two other ranks.
29/30 Aug. R. 22.22 W. 02.50	H.E. and I.B. dropped throughout city with exception of central area. U.X.B. in Hunts Cross area. Gas and water mains damaged. Three Anderson Shelters hit, Dovecot Estate.	16 Sept. R. 19.35 W. 20.55	H.E. damage mainly Great Homer Street. I.B. fell on Carlton Cinema, Moss Lane, but caused no panic among 400 people present. Auxilliary fireman killed, 95, Great Homer Street.
30/31 Aug. R. 22.31 W. 02.48	H.E. and I.B. Everton district, Mill Road Hospital, Coburg Dock. H.E. Brodie Avenue, Sefton Street, slight damage.	17 Sept. R. 15.06 W. 15.42	H.E. dropped near Rootes Aircraft Factory, Speke. Dwelling houses damaged.
31 Aug / 1 Sept. R. 20.48 W. 21.41 R. 23.50 W. 00.00 R. 00.22 W. 03.10	Serious damage by H.E. and I.B. Customs House set on fire. Shelter in Cleveland Square received direct hit. Two cotton warehouses and contents seriously damaged, Stone Street and Vandries Street.	17 Sept. R. 19.48 W. 20.51 R. 22.12 W. 23.51	Widespread severe damage to house property and shops. Church, Lockerby Road, seriously damaged. Eight auxiliary firemen killed in Green Lane, Old Swan, and one policeman fatally injured in Currie Street. Heaviest casualites to date.
3/4 Sept. P. 21.57 R. 22.01 W. 01.17 R. 01.45 W. 03.43	Houses demolished by H.E. in Kensington district. H.E. Lark Lane and Ullet Road area. Incendiary damage Aigburth Vale High School, Lodge Lane Rope Works.	18/19 Sept. R. 19.41 W. 01.04	Heavy damage across city. H.E. hit Walton Prison, trapping several. Railway lines damaged Brownlow Street and St. Michaels Station, Southwood Road. A.T.M. Coy, work impeded for few hours by U.X.B. Nurses' Home, Fazakerley, damaged.
4/5 Sept. R. 21.58 W. 04.23	Mainly H.E. raid directed at Edge Hill Goods Station and Lister Drive Power Station. Surrounding houses damaged but none done to objectives. Dunlop Rubber Works, Tunnel Road Cinema damaged by H.E.	19/20 Sept. R. 19.32 W. 21.02	Walton, Anfield and West Derby districts most affected. A.A. site evacuated due to U.X.B., West Derby. Houses seriously damaged Hilary Road and Rossmore Gardens, West Derby.
5/6 Sept. R. 22.04 W. 03.50	H.E. Claudia Street, Walton. Washington Street and St. James Road badly damaged. Windows of Liverpool Cathedral damaged.	21/22 Sept. R. 19.33 W. 21.05 R. 22.05 W. 04.21	T.J. Hughes store, London Road, seriously damaged by H.E. Mersey Underground Railway penetrated, two trains seriously damaged. Large fires, Warehouses, Alexandra Dock, Byng Street, and timber yard Rimrose Road. East Lancashire Road near Lowerhouse Lane and London Road, Stafford Street to Moss Street, temporarily closed.
6/7 Sept. R. 20.31 W. 01.45	H.E. dropped during daylight. Liver Grease, Oil & Chemical Co., Norfolk Street, gutted by fire. Fourteen A.R.P. ambulances damaged at Milner Safe Works, Smithdown Lane. Liverpool Cathedral windows and stonework damaged.	23/24 Sept. R. 19.51 W. 21.07 R. 22.23 W. 23.48 R. 00.23 W. 04.09	Confined mostly to north part of city. Mainly damage to houses and church, Robson Street, and chapel, Walton Park Cemetery.
10/11 Sept. P. 22.01 R. 22.08 W. 01.26	H.E. West Derby and Woolton districts. House in Speke Road severely damaged. Three U.X.B. in field near Deysbrook Lane A.A. site.	24/25 Sept. P. 02.49 R. 02.50 W. 03.34 R. 04.04 W. 04.27	Serious damage to Cotton Warehouse, Clegg Street, Stanley Tobacco Warehouse, Silcocks Cattle Foodmill, Great Howard Street and Love Lane. Shops in centre of city, Parker Street, Clayton Square and Church Street.
11/12 Sept. R. 22.10 W. 00.54	Oil bomb and H.E. slight damage to a house and telephone wires in Belle Vale Road, Gateacre.	26/27 Sept. R. 19.25 W. 23.40	Extensive damage Wapping, Kings, Queens, Coburg and Brunswick Docks. 13 Warehouses and contents seriously damaged. Fire Brigade Regional Scheme put into operation. Admiralty Store, Canning Place, demolished. Damage to Dock Board and Cunard Buildings by H.E. in Brunswick Street. Tug seriously burnt, Kings Dock.

Warnings	Brief Survey of Incidents	Warnings	Brief Survey of Incidents
27/28 Sept. P. 21.04 R. 21.07 W. 22.08	Houses demolished in Great Homer Street area by H.E. Council School, Banks Road, Garston, damaged.	21/22 Oct. P. 18.51 R. 18.58 W. 02.34	I.B. scattered throughout city. H.E. on Dacy Road, severely damaging dwelling houses. Two tram cars seriously damaged, Priory Road. H.E. on Aigburth Road damaging service mains.
29/30 Sept. R. 22.02 W. 04.00	Mainly I.B. on Everton and Aigburth districts. Oil cake, flax, grain warehouses seriously burnt, Dukes Dock. Two auxiliary firemen killed by falling wall.	25/26 Oct. P. 19.17 R. 19.33 W. 22.03	Three dwelling houses, Richmond Park, demolished by H.E. Serious damage to Holy Trinity School, Richmond Park. Slight fire Mill Lane Rope Works.
1 Oct. P. 19.26 R. 19.35 W. 20.43	I.B. East Toxteth Dock.	26/27 Oct. P. 19.27 R. 19.29 W. 00.58	H.E. of heavy calibre fell in Netherfield Road district, a densely populated area, demolishing three combined shops and dwelling houses and damaging 30 other houses and four public houses, 16 persons trapped, fire greatly impeded rescue work. Majority of those trapped perished. A.R.P. Post demolished, one warden killed, one seriously injured.
7/8 Oct. P. 20.20 R. 20.35 W. 00.20	H.E. Stanley Road, Great Mersey Street, Lichfield Road, Wavertree and Grantley Road, Wavertree. Damage to house property, and Welsh Chapel, Great Mersey Street, demolished.	27/28 Oct. R. 18.01 W. 02.15	First incident about midnight. House property damaged. Serious damage by fire, shed at N.E. Queens Dock, but soon under control. Three of crew of A.F.S. post at Queens Dock killed. Several H.E. on various parts of dock estate only slight damage.
10/11 Oct. R. 18.33 W. 19.54 R. 21.36 W. 23.22	Everton Valley, Knotty Ash, Mossley Hill, Mill Street areas affected in first raid; Anfield district by second raid. Mainly damage to dwelling houses, most serious incidents in Manningham Road and Hogarth Road.	29/30 Oct. R. 11.40 W. 13.04 R. 18.54 W. 19.19 R. 20.07 W. 21.37	First two warnings passed without incident. 20.40 hours, workshops and warehouses, 2 & 4 Thomas Street, demolished by H.E. Superficial damage, windows etc., broken, business premises South Castle Street area. Telephone exchange, South John Street temporarily interrupted service. I.B. Bold Street area, railway sidings, Speke, Matchworks, Garston, etc., small fires resulted in some cases, no serious fire incidents.
11/12 Oct. R. 18.37 W. 19.49 R. 21.00 W. 23.23	City and North Docks attacked in first raid. Severe damage South John Street, James Street, Redcross Street, Paradise Street, Hanover Street, and South Castle Street. H.E. on Alexandra and Langton Docks, causing serious damage to dock sheds, Harbourmaster's house and four ships. Second raid on Hill Street and Bankhall Street areas. Damage to railway track and Admiralty stores.	1/2 Nov. P. 19.46 R. 19.52 W. 21.10 R. 23.52 W. 00.12	I.B. County Road, Great Howard Street, East Lancashire Road districts. Small fires caused slight damage. No incidents during second "alert".
13/14 Oct. P. 21.57 R. 22.14	H.E. on Gladstone and North Hornby Dock. Tenements Myrtle Gardens, hit by two H.E., killing eleven people and injuring nine. Severe damage to dwelling houses Gadsby Street.	4/5 Nov. P. 19.49 R. 19.54 W. 20.48 R. 00.39 W. 01.28 R. 03.42 W. 04.02	H.E. Townsend Avenue, Wavertree Playground during first alert, two houses seriously damaged, 15 slightly damaged, fractured gas main took fire but fire was extinguished by water from burst water main. No casualties. No incidents during second and third "alerts".
16 Oct. P. 19.03 R. 19.24 W. 21.10	I.B. on Walton and Everton districts. Surface shelters, Louisa Street, hit, causing about 30 casualties.	8/9 Nov. Six "alerts" P. 19.23 R. 19.24 W. 20.53	Only incidents occurred during period 19.50-20.00 hours. I.B. dropped in Childwall Valley Road area. Only damage at North Farm, Wambo Lane, which was slight.
17/18 Oct. P. 21.12 R. 21.19 W. 22.39	West wing Fazakerley Sanatorium demolished, and one patient killed. H.E. damage to dwelling houses West Derby. U.X.B. yard of Morrison School.	12 Nov. P. 19.55 R. 20.05 W. 21.21	Oil incendiary on roof of Post Office, 2/4 Wavertree Road, slight damage to roof. Four H.E. within radius of half a mile of Edge Hill Railway Goods station. Three dwelling houses demolished, several slightly damaged. Balloon barrage not operating owing to high wind and raiders flew at low altitude.
18 Oct. P. 19.51 R. 19.54 W. 22.51	H.E. damage mainly confined to dwelling houses Norris Green and southern part of city. St. Clement's Church, Beaumont Street, seriously damaged.	18 Nov. P. 02.39 R. 02.52 W. 03.56	I.B. house Guest Street and warehouse Sefton Street. Slight damage. No casualties. A number of balloons came down in flames, apparently caused by atmospheric conditions. No H.E.
19 Oct. P. 18.49 R. 19.00 W. 23.56	H.E. Tuebrook district and southern portion of city. Dwelling houses and shops, High Park Street, demolished. St. Silas' Church, St. Silas Street, severely damaged. G.2 Report and Control Centre, Seamen's Orphanage, Orphan Drive, hit by H.E. which failed to explode, causing damage.	18/19 Nov. P. 19.32 R. 19.43 W. 22.52	Large number of I.B. in Aigburth district, followed by H.E. Slight damage by fire to numerous dwelling houses, two schools and a church. H.E. demolished the houses 3/5 Wingate Road. Other H.E. caused serious damage to houses and a school in the Aigburth area. Later in the Anfield area three houses were demolished and numerous houses damaged. The houses 68a, 70a, and 70 Teulon Street, were demolished. Many houses in this area damaged.
21 Oct. R. 07.28 W. 07.46	H.E. dropped near Rootes Aircraft Factory, Speke, causing slight damage to overhead electric wires.	22/23 Nov. P. 21.40 R. 22.50 W. 23.04	H.E. in Great George Street district at 22.40 hours. Slight damage to houses, shops and other business premises.

Warnings	Brief Survey of Incidents	Warnings	Brief Survey of Incidents
28/29 Nov. P. 19.03 R. 19.23 W. 03.58	Heaviest raid to date. Commenced with I.B. followed by H.E. and P.M. P.M. on Botanic Park and Durning Road, basement shelter hit. Estimated 290 people in shelter at the time. 166 dead were finally recovered. Damage caused in Rose Place and district to dwelling houses and a cinema, P.M. in Commercial Road. P.M. were also responsible for fires and damage to Spofforth Road Gas Works, and a sugar shed in Garston Docks. Considerable damage in Holland Street and Ardleigh Road districts. Allerton, Wavertree and Childwall districts received I.B. 30 P.M. dropped in area, eight of which failed to explode.	9/10 Jan. P. 19.34 R. 19.37 W. 01.18	H.E. on South docks and Dingle oil depot. Serious damage South Herculaneum and slight damage to oil depot. I.B. were dropped on the outer districts of the city, but damage caused by these was in the main slight. Number of houses demolished in Virgil Street by H.E. Slight fires and damage caused by I.B. in Everton district. Dutch barn burnt out at Holt Farm, Gateacre. Police Stores, Everton Terrace, roof penetrated by I.B., which fell on uniform clothing. Slight damage.
29/30 Nov. P. 22.35 R. 22.39 W. 23.50	Raid of short duration, mainly confined to Rathbone Road area. H.E. in use, little damage. I.B. caused slight fires.	15/16 Feb. R. 13.39 W. 13.49 R. 19.34 W. 20.08 R. 23.23 W. 02.06	No incidents during first alert. During second, number of I.B. dropped in Aigburth Vale area. Slight damage during third period. H.E. and I.B. dropped on north end of city. G.P.O. garage, Commercial Road demolished. Other damage, slight.
20/21 Dec. P. 18.19 R. 18.20 W. 03.58	Attack opened with I.B. followed by H.E. and P.M. Extensive fires broke out causing considerable damage. Fires caused by I.B. in Town Hall, Municipal Buildings, and Cunard Offices and at Landing Stage. Nine men killed in P.M. incident at Waterloo Dock. P.M. exploded near Adelphi Hotel, causing considerable damage to surrounding property. North Docks hit by many H.E.	12/13 Mar. P. 20.27 R. 19.13 W. 19.23 R. 20.29 W. 03.56	No incidents during first alert. During the night the city was heavily attacked, and 126 fires were dealt with by the Fire Brigade and A.F.S. Serious fires at Head Post Office, Victoria Street, South John Street Telephone Exchange, Municipal Annexe, Dale Street, and numerous other buildings in centre of town. Assistance was rendered by outside fire brigades in view of scale of attack. Entire organisation worked faultlessly.
21/22 Dec. P. 18.31 R. 18.38 W. 05.15	Large numbers of I.B. used in opening phase, causing many fires, a great number serious. Assistance had to be called for by Fire Services. Several shelters hit with resultant casualties. Raid was longest experienced in Liverpool. Notable incidents were St George's Hall and Fish Market, Hatton Garden and Electric Station at Highfield Street, Hanover Street (Messrs. Ayrton Saunders hit by H.E.), and severe fire at Messrs. Goodlass Walls (Paint Establishment). Prescot Street Police Station damaged by P.M. and nearby bedding factory was demolished. Other P.M. fell in the vicinity, damaging Royal Infirmary and demolishing dwelling houses. P.M. caused havoc in "D" and "G" Divisions; outstanding incident being fire at a R.N. establishment in Melias' Building, Love Lane. H.E. and I.B. damage in Canada, Gladstone, Brocklebank, Princes, Wapping, Kings and Carriers Docks.	13/14 Mar. P. 20.25 R. 20.33 W. 02.14	Attack on City not heavy. H.E. caused extensive damage at S.3 Alexandra Dock shed. Other H.E. dropped on other parts of city caused only slight damage. Two ships sank in river during afternoon of 13th March, after striking mines.
22/23 Dec. P. 18.31 R. 18.38 W. 06.12	H.E. and I.B. cause one death at 7/9 Medlock Street. Six people killed by H.E. at Garage in Ensor Street, and at 2 Huskisson Dock Shed. Serious damage caused in latter incident. Another death resulted by H.E. on a vessel in Canada Tongue; Langton and Alexandra Docks received slight damage. Messrs. Rootes received a hit by H.E. on a shelter, causing one death and three seriously injured.	14/15 Mar. R. 20.52 W. 02.36	About 200 I.B. fell in Speke district, causing slight damage by fire to houses and a factory. Later nine H.E. were dropped near Kirkdale Railway Station. Four fell on the sidings and caused serious damage to the permanent way, railway coaches, etc.
23/24 Dec. R. 19.08 W. 01.23	H.E. were reported to have fallen in the river opposite the Brunswick Half-tide Dock.	7/8 April P. 21.17 R. 21.35 W. 03.45	About 20 exposive I.B. fell in Beaconsfield Road area, 150 in Garston and 200 in Menlove Avenue district. Large number of I.B. fell in Lister Drive area, some on electric power station, but damage slight. H.E. fell in Edge Lane area, demolishing church and seriously damaging convent. No casualties.
1/2 Jan 1941. P. 21.06 R. 21.11 W. 01.51	No. 11 Redcross Street, a sack warehouse, was demolished by H.E. and damage caused in Mercer Court. H.E. reported in the river near Brunswick Dock. A suspected P.M. fell in the river outside the Brunswick Dock, causing considerable damage.	15/16 April P. 21.58 R. 23.00 W. 04.03	Garston and Aigburth districts attacked with I.B., some explosive. Resulting fires only minor. Later H.E. demolished dwelling houses 42 and 44 Saunby Street, Garston, and eight persons were killed there. Serious damage to other houses in neighbourhood. Later H.E. dropped in Gt. Homer Street area, causing much damage to houses. H.E. in other parts of city did not cause much damage. Several U.X.B. in Garston area.
3/4 Jan. P. 19.10 R. 19.14 W. 19.47	Single plane dropped I.B. on Sandforth Road district and Newsham Park allotments. Only damage caused was to an empty stable in Sandforth Road, where a small fire started.	26/27 April P. 22.18 R. 22.27 W. 01.59	Most damage caused by P.M. dropped between Townsend Avenue and Muirhead Avenue. Centre of city only slightly affected. I.B. fell on several districts causing slight damage. H.E. dropped in Wayville Close, Allerton, causing serious damage to houses. P.M. fell in Ballantyne Road, causing extensive damage and many casualties. Several U.X.B. and U.X.P.M. in Ballantyne Road.

Warnings	Brief Survey of Incidents

Warnings	Brief Survey of Incidents

1/2 May
P. 22.30
R. 22.34   W. 00.28
	"A" Div - Serious H.E. damage to Cooked Meat Factory, New Bird Street. Timber yard, Kempston Street, shop, 85 London Road, glass roof, Lime Street station.
	    "B" Div - H.E. on Low Hill district caused damage to house property.
	    "C" Div - Serious damage to houses, Grafton Street and shed, West Brunswick Dock.
	    "D" Div - Houses and shop, Cazneau Street area.
	    "E" Div - Nil.
	    "F" Div - Damage to railway line near Speke Road Bridge. Houses, Claremont Road, Garmoyle Road, Wellington Road demolished.
	    "G" Div - Very serious fire at Crawfords' Biscuit Works, Binns Road.

2/3 May
P. 22.15
R. 22.20   W. 02.37
	Serious fire damage to warehouses and contents in Bridgewater Street, Norfolk Street and Chaloner Street; dock sheds N.E. Queens Dock, Mersey Docks and Harbour Board, Corn Exchange, Rice Mill, Upper Pownall Street, Gas Company's works, Duke Street.
	    "A" Div - P.M. South Castle Street – serious damage to shops, two tram cars, and Queen's Dock Gate Passage electric sub-station, Dock Road completely blocked, Overhead Railway collapsed. H.E. Lumber Street, rear Exchange Railway Station. Serious damage to surrounding office and shop property and railway station. P.M. Cornwallis Street, serious damage to dwelling houses. Strand Street, James Street, large fires and heavy damage. Blast damage to India Buildings, Cunard Building, Tunnel Building.
	    "B" Div - Dwelling houses, shops, Upper Huskisson Street, Bedford Street, London Road, Pembroke Place, seriously damaged.
	    "C" Div - P.M. caused heavy damage to houses, Linnet Lane, Ullet Road, Waverley Road, Mannering Road, Coltart Road and Kingsley Road. H.E. on Brunswick Goods Station. Wapping Overhead Railway Station, Grafton Street and Buckland Street.
	    "D" Div - St. Brigid's Church and Crypt (air raid shelter) partially demolished.
	    "E" Div - H.E. on St. Athanasius Church, Fountains Road and houses, Chancel Street. P.M. Hunslet Road, Donsby Road, railway signal works, Adlam Crescent.
	    "F" Div - P.M. Bowland Avenue, Maple Grove, Egerton Road, Ministry of Pensions Hospital, Park Avenue, Ibbotsons Lane and Smithdown Road Cemetery; all caused extensive damage. H.E. damage in Ullet Road, Glenconner Road, Childwall Valley Road, Fern Grove, Childwall Abbey Road, also serious.
	    "G" Div - P.M. on Pemberton Road caused extensive damage to houses and Old Swan Police Station suffered from blast. Oil I.B. caused damage to Automatic Telephone Company factory, Binns Road.

3/4 May P. 22.24 R. 22.30 W. 04.50	Most devastating raid yet. Gas, water and electric mains seriously affected. Central telephone exchange cut off. "A" Div - Lewis's and Blacklers' Stores gutted by fire. Area bounded by Lord Street, Paradise Street, Canning Place, devastated. Wolstenholme Square; Leyton Paper Mills, Henry Street; Tatler Cinema, Church Street; Salvage Corps, Hatton Garden; Head Post Office; Littlewoods Building, Hanover Street; Government Buildings, Crosshall Street; Museum and Library, William Brown Street; Magistrates' Court; Custom House; Central Railway Station; India Buildings; Central Telephone Exchange, South John Street, all seriously damaged. Large fires caused damage at Princes Dock, Riverside Station, Dukes Dock, Canning Dock, Salthouse Dock, E. Wapping Basin, Stewarts' Warehouse, Gower Street, and S.S. Clan McInness, N. King's No. 2 Dock.

Warnings	Brief Survey of Incidents

	"B" Div - P.M. Mill Road Infirmary - many casualties and much damage.
	    "C" Div - 17 houses demolished in Alt Street.
	    "D" Div - Basement shelter, Gildarts Gardens; shelter Addison Street Schools; shelter, Anthony Street, and basement shelter, Vulcan Street, hit by H.E. Rose Hill Police Station damaged.
	    "E" Div - P.M. in Hermia Street, Stanley Road, Carisbrooke Road, Fountains Road, Newman Street, Freeland Street, Index Street, Margaret Road, Peter Road and Dallas Grove, caused extensive damage and many casualties. Two wings of H.M. Prison demolished, Kirkdale Railway station hit. H.E. caused serious damage to shops in Kirkdale and Walton areas. Fires caused serious damage to Kinross Mill, Tillotsons Paper and Printing Works, Walton Parish Church destroyed and Walton Police Station slightly damaged. Docks seriously damaged by P.M. and H.E. One ship, S.S. Malakand, loaded with ammunition was set on fire and exploded at about 09.00 hours, 4th May, causing widespread damage in which several barges and a coaster were sunk. Police refreshment room destroyed.
	    "F" Div - Sudley Road Council School, Rose Lane Council School and Corporation yard Smithdown Road, seriously damaged.
	    "G" Div - Serious fire, Breckside Corporation depot, underground shelter; Queens Drive, Edge Lane Drive, hit.
	    Ammunition train set on fire at Breck Road railway siding, with resultant damage to house property over a wide area.
	    Anfield Road School and Leyfield School suffered extensive damage.

4/5 May
P. 23.55
R. 23.58   W. 04.26
	"A" Div - Belgian Seamen's Hotel, Great George Street, hit by H.E.
	    "B" Div - Houses demolished, Catharine Street, Fairy Street, Mountjoy Street and Magnum Street.
	    "C" Div - Serious damage to Clinic, Northumberland Street.
	    "D" Div - St. Silvester's School and Rotunda Theatre destroyed by fire. Gas Works, Athol Street, received direct hit, demolishing one holder; Hadfield's Fertiliser Works badly damaged.
	    "E" Div - Walton Lane School seriously damaged by P.M.
	    "F" Div - Nil.
	    "G" Div - Four houses demolished in Bingley Road.

6 May
P. 23.59
R. 00.03   W. 04.07
	"A" Div - Serious damage by H.E. to St. Nicholas' Church; Warehouse, Lancelots Hey; Salvation Army Hostel, Park Lane; 52 South Castle Street; Dukes Grain Warehouse, West King's Dock Quay, and South Canning Dock; Chemical Works, Hardy Street and Park Lane; Great George Street Congregational Church; St. Luke's Church and surrounding property; Gas Office, Duke Street.
	    "B" Div - Serious damage to No. 2 Ward, Royal Infirmary; Nurses' Home, Mulberry Street; St. Silas' Church, Pembroke Place; T.J. Hughes, London Road.
	    "C" Div - Tenements, Northumberland Street; dwelling houses, Lodge Lane area, and dining room, Coburg Dock Avenue, severely damaged by H.E.
	    "D" Div - Public house, Christian Street, demolished. Emido Flour Mills, Glasgow Street, seriously damaged.
	    "E" Div - Nil.
	    "F" Div - Serious damage, dwelling houses Harvey Street and Smithdown Road.
	    "G" Div - Nil.
	    Fires were extensive, the more serious being in Renshaw Street, Duke Street area. Salt water mains were used to a great extent. Slight fire at Liverpool Cathedral. Whole area around Bold Street and Colquitt Street was considerably involved in fire.

Warnings	Brief Survey of Incidents
6/7 May P. 23.50 R. 23.53 W. 04.07	"A" Div - H.E. damage to Parcel Post Office, Hatton Garden; Town Hall (slight). Landing Stage and Ferry Goods Stage also damaged. Serious fires at the Custom House and Bent's Brewery, Johnson Street. "B" Div - H.E. Kensington district demolished several houses. St. Catharine's Church, Abercromby Square, was destroyed by fire. "C" Div - Damage sustained at Mill Street Police Station due to I.B. Serious fire damage to Wilson's Flour Mills, Mill Street; East Harrington Shed. West Harrington Shed, South Coburg Shed; service pipe line at Dingle Jetty. Police hut, N.E. Brunswick Dock, demolished by H.E. H.E. on Brunswick Gardens tenements and Cheshire Lines Committee Goods Station. "D" Div - H.E. on Overhead Railway damaged permanent way. Ships in Bramley Moor Dock seriously damaged and two barges in South Stanley Dock sunk. Engineering works, Charters Street, gutted by fire. "E" Div - Nil. "F" Div - Nil. "G" Div - Damage to a number of dwelling houses due to faulty A.A. shells which exploded on falling.
7/8 May P. 23.57 R. 00.02 W. 04.25	Heavy damage throughout city by H.E., I.B. and Oil I.B. "A" Div - Serious damage to Tower Building, Water Street; Morris & Jones' Warehouse, Sir Thomas Street, and damage to serivce mains by H.E. Tram car damaged by H.E., Pier Head. "B" Div - Workshop, Pembroke Place, and Builders' yard, Fairclough Lane, gutted by fire. "C" Div - Nil. "D" Div - Serious fires, Cooperage, Gildarts Gardens, and stables, Dickson Street. Surface shelters demolished, Beatrice Street and Norris Street. A.F.S. pump and Lancashire County Police Mobile Canteen destroyed. Many dwelling houses, Scotland Road area, demolished. Damage widespread throughout division. "E" Div - P.M. Sandholme Street. P.M. Teulon Street destroyed dwelling houses and three air-raid shelters. Serious damage throughout division, churches, schools destroyed. Rolling stock, Bankhall Carriage Sidings destroyed. Stanley Road bridge over railway smashed. Warehouse, Townsend Street, demolished. Serious damage to Sandon Motor Works, Grundy Street. A.F.S. Station, Forth Street; Lambeth Road School; Distillery, Juniper Street; Shelter, Townsend Street; B&A Tobacco Factory, Commercial Road; Carnarvon Road and Rice Lane, Walton Hospital. Serious damage to North Docks, sheds and railway sheds; three ships sunk. "F" Div - P.M. on Daffodil Road caused serious damage to swelling houses. "G" Div - Nil.
29 May P. 00.49 R. 00.51 W. 03.53	H.E. was dropped in two districts, causing damage to growing wheat in Croxteth Estate, and damage to an Army Unit nearby. Eight dwelling houses sustained damage in the Beaumont Street area.
31 May P. 00.33 R. 01.00 W. 03.30	I.B. damage, N. Coburg Dock. N.W. Toxteth Dock, N.E. Brunswick Dock and Coburg Grain Warehouse. H.E. damaged an electric main in Stanley Park Avenue and a water pipe in Pinehurst Avenue. Two houses damaged in a previous raid demolished by H.E.
1 June P. 00.36 R. 00.37 W. 03.12	I.B. caused slight fires on the Gladstone Dock area but no damage. H.E. also fell in this area, causing some damage to the masonry adjoining the Lock and to Naval Stores at N.W. Gladstone Shed. Damage also sustained at No. 3 Alexandra Dock Quay, N.W. Hornby shed by fire. H.E. fell in County Road and Breeze Hill, damaging three houses.
25 June P. 01.11 R. 01.12 W. 03.35	Two H.E. demolished a hut in a nursery in Mackets Lane, and another on the locomotives in sheds at N.E. Princes Dock, causing considerable damage. Damage also sustained at West Waterloo Dock. I.B. in the Rose Hill area caused fires in a church and a disused dwelling. An A.A. shell caused damage to aircraft at Linner Road, Speke. No casualties reported.
24 July P. 01.21 R. 01.27 W. 03.17	A.A. Shells caused damage to dwelling houses in the north end of the city, in County Road and Everton districts.
22 Oct. P. 20.45 R. 20.51 W. 23.57	No incidents by enemy action. Damage was caused by A.A. shells in "A" Division and "F" Division.
1 Nov. P. 21.04 R. 21.07 W. 23.02	H.E. dropped on a cottage in a wood on Croxteth Estate, slight damage, and an A.A. nose cap caused slight damage to 27 Lomond Road.
10 Jan 1942. P. 22.49 R. 22.57 W. 01.15	H.E. dropped in "C" Division, causing damage to houses in Stanhope Street and Upper Stanhope Street, and demolished Nos. 111/119 Upper Stanhope Street.

Under the Fire Brigade's Regional Reinforcement Scheme, Fire Brigades of the following towns were called in to assist the Liverpool Fire Service:

Accrington, Altrincham, Arnold, Ashton-under-Lyne, Atherton, Bacup, Barnoldswick, Barnsley, Birmingham, Blackburn, Blackpool, Bolsover, Bradford, Bulwell, Burnley, Burton-on-Trent, Bury, Buxton, Carlton, Castleford, Chester, Chesterfield, Chorley, Cleethorpes, Clown, Colwyn Bay, Connahs Quay, Conisborough, Coventry, Crosby, Denton, Derby, Dewsbury, Doncaster, Dukinfield, Eccles, Eston, Featherstone, Flint, Formby, Frodsham, Gainsborough, Glossop, Grantham, Grimsby, Halifax, Harrogate, Hawarden, Heywood, Heanor, Hinckley, Holmfirth, Holywell, Hucknall, Huddersfield, Huyton-with-Roby, Hyde, Irlam, Keighley, Knutsford, Leeds, Leicester, Leigh, Lichfield, Lincoln, Litherland, London, Long Eaton, Loughborough, Manchester, Mansfield, Mexborough, Middleton, Mirfield, Mold, Morley, Nelson, Newcastle-under-Lyme, Newton-le-Willows, Nottingham, Oldham, Oswestry, Pontefract, Prescot, Prestatyn, Preston, Pudsey, Rawtenstall, Rochdale, Rotherham, Rothwell, Runcorn, Sale, Salford, Scunthorpe, Sheffield, Shipley, Shrewsbury, Southport, Sowerby Bridge, Spenborough, St Helens, Stoke, Stretford, Sutton Coldfield, Swinton and Pendlebury, Tamworth, Thornaby-on-Tees, Thorne, Urmston, Wakefield, Warrington, West Bridgeford, West Bromwich, West Hartlepool, Whiston, Wigan, Wilmslow, Wombwell, Worksop, Wortley, Wrexham, York.

Strength of the Force

To meet the extra calls on the Police due to the war, the establishment was increased by (1) appointing pensioned officers as first Police Reserves, (2) appointment of men to the Police War Reserve, and (3) appointment of women to the Women's Auxiliary Police Corps.

The total number of air-raid warnings, "Red" (Alert), received in Liverpool was 509.

During the raids, a total of 2,596 persons were killed, 2,548 were seriously injured, of whom 154 subsequently died, and 1,600 were slightly injured.